36835000039765

TITLE IV. B
PLACED AT

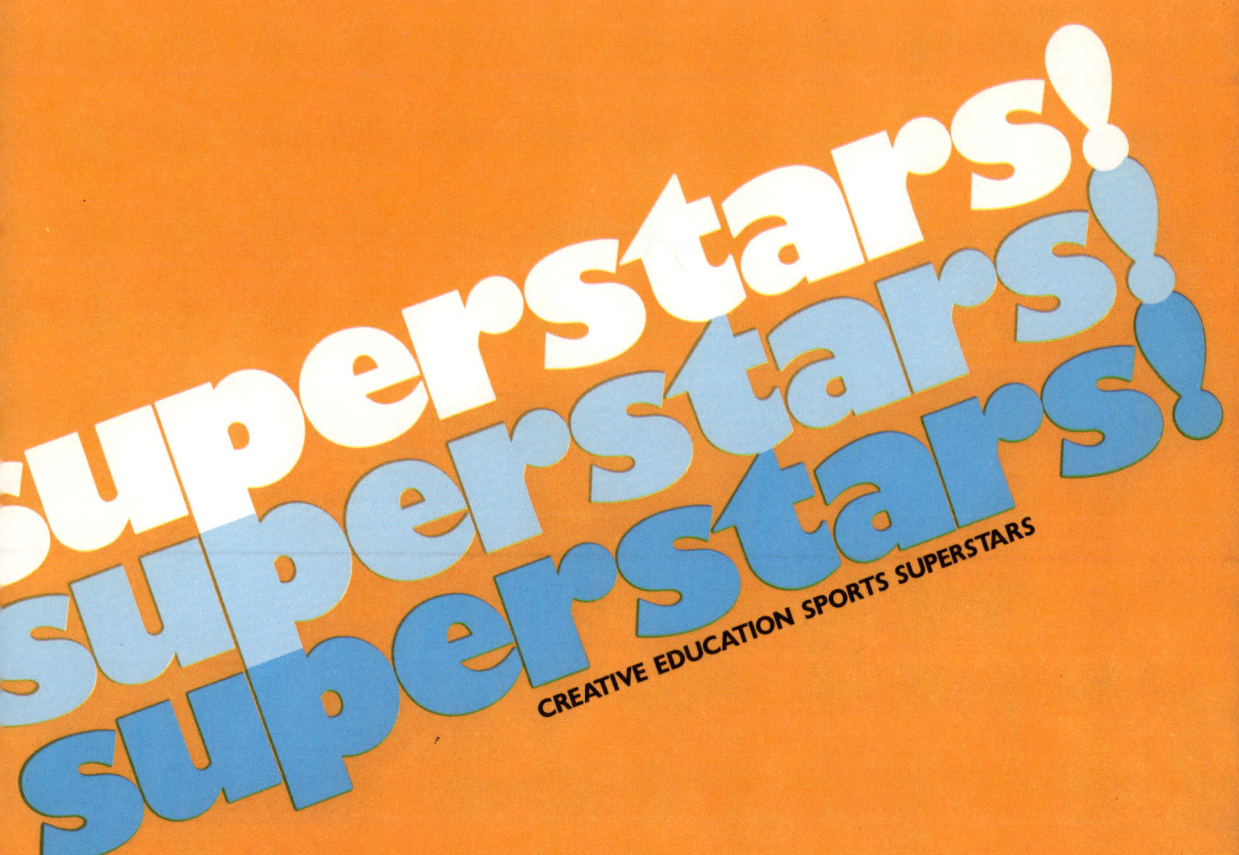

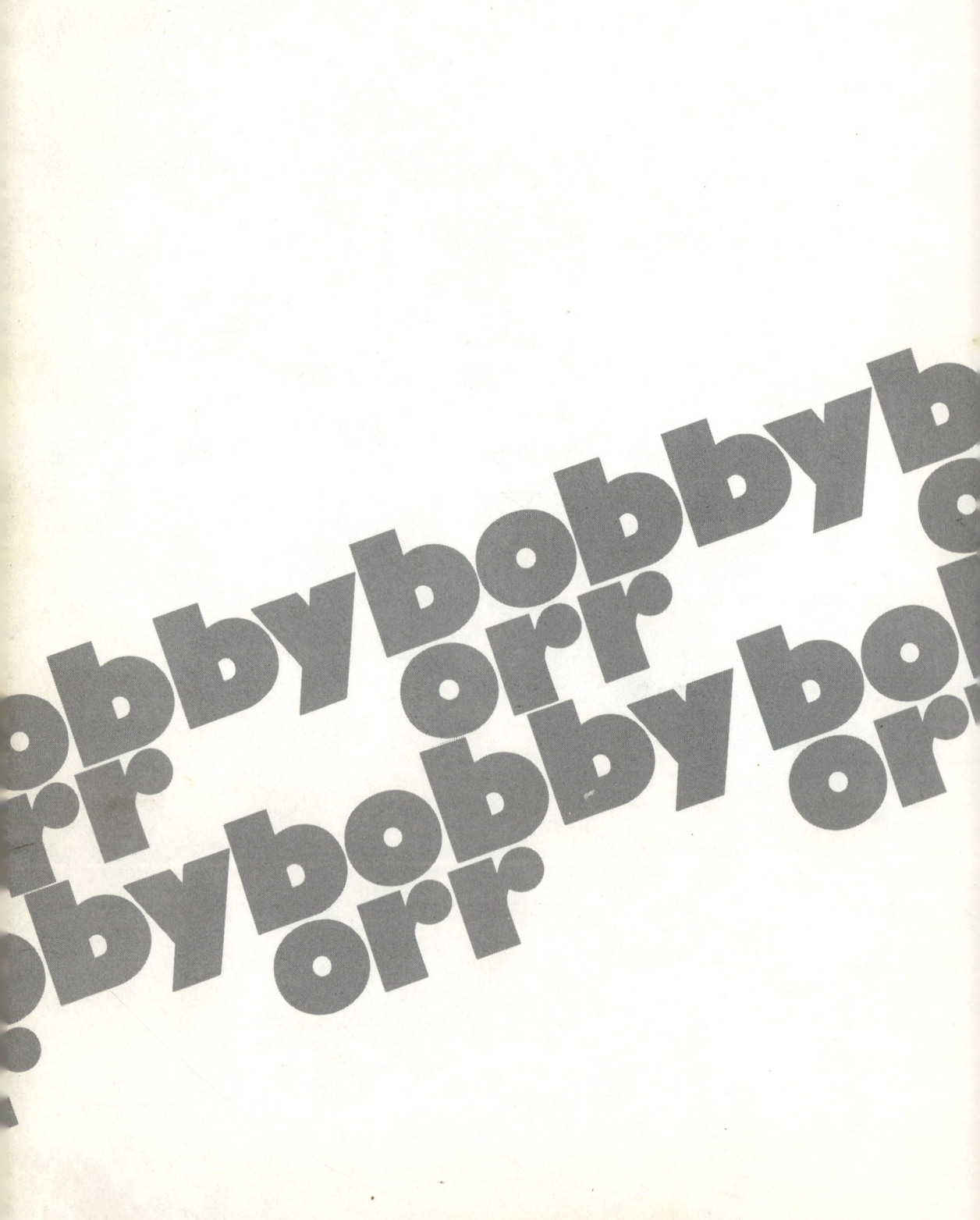

bobby orr

by Jay H. Smith
illustrated by Harold Henriksen

CREATIVE EDUCATION
MANKATO, MINNESOTA

Published by Creative Education, 123 South Broad Street, P. O. Box 227, Mankato, Minnesota 56001

Copyright © 1974 by Creative Education. International copyrights reserved in all countries. No part of this book may be reproduced in any form without written permission from the publisher. Printed in the United States.

Distributed by Childrens Press, 1224 West Van Buren Street, Chicago, Illinois 60607

Cover: Sports Illustrated photo by Tony Triolo © Time, Inc.

Library of Congress Number: 74-8848 ISBN: 0-87191-368-2

Library of Congress Cataloging in Publication Data
Smith, Jay H
  Bobby Orr.
  SUMMARY: A biography of the Canadian boy who from the age of fourteen was primed to lead the Boston Bruins out of their losing streak into NHL victory.
  1. Orr, Bobby, 1948- —Juvenile literature. [1. Orr, Bobby, 1948- 2. Hockey—Juvenile literature. 2. Hockey—Biography] I. Henriksen, Harold, illus. II. Title.
GV848.5.O7S58   796.9'62'0924 [B] [92]   74-8848
ISBN 0-87191-368-2

Bobby Orr's exploits on the ice have won the hearts of Boston hockey fans. Perhaps no other athlete has ever meant so much to a city as Bobby Orr means to Boston.

To Bostonians the Bruin defenseman is more than a brilliant hockey player. He is perhaps the city's most popular resident. His name is magic. Thousands of cars throughout the Boston area bear bumper stickers which read "This is Orr Country" and "God Bless Orr Country."

Whenever Bobby Orr leads the Bruins onto the ice at the Boston Garden, the atmosphere is charged with excitement. A Bruin victory produces intense joy among rabid Boston fans.

In such moments of frenzy Bostonians are inclined to forget their rich historical tradition for awhile. They might say then that the most memorable event in Boston's glorious past was not the Boston Tea Party of 1773, but the night Bobby Orr played his first home game in 1966.

Boston's love affair with Bobby Orr began even before he put on a Bruin uniform. Bruin fans first heard his name in 1962 when Bobby was only 14.

The Bruins had failed to make the National Hockey League (NHL) playoffs for 3 straight years. During the 1960-61 and 1961-62 seasons they had finished dead last. Not only were the Bruins bad, they seemed to have no hope for the future. The fans were totally discouraged.

Then they began to hear about Bobby Orr, an amateur hockey wizard playing for the Oshawa Generals, a Bruin farm club in the Ontario Hockey Association.

In desperation, Bruin fans began to place all their hopes on this virtually unknown boy. They knew it would be 4 long years before Bobby would be 18 and thus old enough to play in the NHL. That didn't dampen their enthusiasm at all.

The history of hockey is full of stories about promising junior players who blazed like meteors for a time and then were heard of no more. Still, the most stubborn Bruin

fans refused to believe that this would ever happen to Bobby.

Things went from bad to worse for Boston during the next 3 years. They played ragged, uninspired hockey, always finishing last. In order to keep a spark of enthusiasm alive, Bruin owners constantly reminded the fans of Bobby's progress at Oshawa. The development of their prodigy had been spectacular.

During his last year at Oshawa, the town's newspaper carried advertisements which read: "See Boston's $1,000,000 Prospect, Bobby Orr!"

Enthusiasm ran even higher in Boston. General Manager Hap Emms said he wouldn't trade Bobby for the entire Toronto Maple Leaf team. Another Bruin official declared he wouldn't take $2,000,000 for Bobby.

As the 1966-67 season approached, the pressure on Bobby was tremendous. Although he had not yet played a single NHL game, Bobby was being heralded as an instant star. Bobby knew that the fans would expect miracles from him almost every game.

Another thing bothered Bobby. His contract called for a bigger salary than that of most of his teammates. Bobby worried that they would resent him for this. In training camp, however, the Bruins quickly accepted him as a member of the team.

One day in practice Bobby put on a dazzling display of skating and stick-handling. Then veteran defenseman Ted Green skated over to Bobby and said, "I don't know how much money you're getting, kid; but it isn't enough."

Bobby was nervous before his first NHL game at Detroit against the Red Wings. He said later, "This was my big night. This was what I was waiting for—the NHL."

The NHL was also waiting for Bobby. The Red Wings were eager to test the rookie. They wanted to see whether he'd be afraid to fight back.

Gordie Howe, one of hockey's all-time greats, gave Bobby a hard 2-handed slap with his stick across the gloves. Another Red Wing hit Bobby in the stomach with his stick. But now Bobby started to fight back. He played well, assisting on 1 goal in Boston's 6 to 2 victory.

Then the moment Boston fans had been awaiting for came at last. In his first home game Bobby scored a brilliant goal on a long slapshot from the blue line. The sell-out crowd in the Boston Garden gave Bobby a standing ovation which lasted for several minutes. The wildest dreams of the Bruin fans were beginning to come true.

Robert Gordon Orr was born on March 20, 1948, in Parry Sound, Ontario, Canada. During the long winters the temperature sometimes drops to 40 degrees below zero. The Seguin River is frozen solid from mid-December to April. It is the kind of town that produces the best hockey players.

Bobby is lucky he ever got a chance to play hockey at all. When Bobby was born, his parents were told that the baby might not live. But in a few hours Bobby gained strength and was soon healthy enough to leave the hospital.

Shortly after he learned to walk, Bobby began to imitate the older boys in Parry Sound. He would slide around in his rubber boots on an ice-covered road with a hockey stick in his small hands, pretending he was playing hockey.

When he was 4, Bobby was given his first pair of skates. At first his ankles were too weak to support him. He spent hours stumbling across the ice.

Before long, Bobby was skating well. He began to play shinny, a popular Canadian keep-away game. There were no teams. It was every boy for himself. The idea of the game is for a player to get the puck and keep it for as long as he can. It seemed that Bobby always had the puck. Nobody ever seemed to catch him. Playing shinny taught Bobby a great deal.

By the time he was 5, Bobby was ready to play organized hockey with the local Minor Squirt team. It didn't take long before people began to take notice of Bobby's instinctive ability.

Hardly anyone in Parry Sound was surprised. Doug Orr, Bobby's father, had been an outstanding player himself. At 17 Doug Orr had attracted major league scouts, eager to sign him to a contract.

But the Second World War was on then. Doug Orr decided to join the Canadian Navy. When he returned home at 21, Doug Orr's chance to play pro hockey was gone.

He and Arva Orr were beginning to raise their young family. Doug Orr needed the security of a steady job. He went to work at a Parry Sound factory.

Doug Orr was very proud of Bobby. He sometimes worked the night shift so he could see Bobby play in the afternoons.

Bobby practiced all the time during his early years. By the time he was 12, his coaches decided that Bobby was too good to play against boys his own age. Bobby advanced to the Bantam team and skated with boys of 14. Although he was only 5-feet-2 and weighed just 110 pounds, Bobby was the star of the team.

After the season ended, the team was invited to play in the Bantam Championship of Ontario at Gananoque, 300 miles away.

One of the spectators at Gananoque was a Boston Bruin scout named Wren Blair, later General Manager of the Minnesota North Stars. "I was there," Blair has said, "to watch a couple of Gananoque boys, Rick Eaton and Doug Higgins. As soon as I saw this Parry Sound kid in droopy pants in charge of the game, I forgot Eaton and Higgins."

"He made so many good moves so easily," Blair said, "that I figured we had to get him for the Bruins."

Boston then began a secret campaign to obtain the future rights to Bobby Orr. Negotiations had to be conducted in secrecy because the Bruins feared that another NHL club would try to take Bobby away from them.

Blair went to Parry Sound and discovered that the town's amateur hockey program was unsponsored. The

Bruins then donated $1,000 a year for the next 3 years to the local hockey association. Blair also visited the Orr family frequently. He soon won their respect.

When Bobby was 14, Blair visited the Orrs again. He suggested that Bobby attend a summer tryout camp for junior players at Niagara Falls. Players who did well there would be offered a chance to play for the Bruins' farm club at Oshawa.

Doug and Arva Orr didn't want Bobby to go. He would be competing against 18-year-olds, some of whom would outweigh Bobby by more than 50 pounds. But they let Bobby make his own decision. He was eager to go.

When Bobby appeared at the camp, the other players were startled. He looked too little to belong there. They soon learned otherwise. Of the 75 players at the camp, Bobby was clearly the best.

Then Wren Blair tried to convince the Orrs to let Bobby play for Oshawa. At first they refused. They didn't believe Bobby was ready for such a big jump. But Blair persisted. At last, a compromise was reached.

Bobby would continue to live at home, commuting to Oshawa only when the team played its games, which was usually twice a week. He would not be allowed to make the 300-mile round trip every day to practice with the team.

The Orrs also stipulated that Bobby would quit the club if his health or school grades suffered.

At first Bobby's Oshawa teammates resented the fact that he was allowed to miss practice. They found it hard to believe that a 14-year-old could be that good. Newspapermen began to write glowing stories about hockey's new whiz kid.

Another boy might have found the pressure of excessive publicity and the jealousy of his teammates too much to overcome, but the problem never seemed to affect Bobby very much. He accepted the situation in an amazingly grown-up manner.

When the season ended, Bobby was named to the Second All-Star team. Wren Blair was pleased. "Imagine if he had been able to practice with the team," he said.

The following year Bobby went to live in Oshawa.

Doug and Arva Orr were criticized by their neighbors for letting Bobby go, but the Orrs felt sure their son was mature enough to conduct himself well. Bobby never let them down.

During his 3 years in Oshawa Bobby lived with families who treated him like their own son. He called home often and went back to Parry Sound whenever he could. In the summers Bobby came home to be with his family.

By the time he was 16, Bobby had completely mastered the basic skills of stick-handling, skating, passing and shooting. Oshawa Coach Jim Cherry said, "It's almost as if he has a magnet at the end of his stick, the way he attracts the puck."

Bobby became an idol in Oshawa. The city was crazy about the handsome young star. Bobby hardly ever read what newspaper reporters wrote about him. "I try not to read about myself," he said. "So many people have told me not to get a swelled head that I'm scared to read the stuff."

Bobby's record at Oshawa was outstanding. He scored 30, 34 and 37 goals in his last 3 seasons, setting and breaking a new league mark for defensemen every year. He made the First All-Star team all 3 campaigns.

Bobby was now ready for the NHL. Boston fans were anxiously awaiting the player they were already calling

Super Boy.

Bobby's rookie season was even better than Bruin fans had hoped for. He thrilled them with his daring skating. Occasionally Bobby took a chance that backfired and was caught out of position—allowing the opposing team to score an easy goal. But Bobby learned from his mistakes, seldom making the same one twice.

Boston fans overlooked Bobby's momentary lapses. This was a rare thing for them to do. Bruin fans are notoriously fickle. They'll usually boo a player for a single mistake, even when he's played sensationally all the game. Throughout Bobby's career Bruin fans never did this to him.

Bobby finished the 1966-67 season with 13 goals and 28 assists. He was named to the Second All-Star team and was awarded the Calder Trophy as the NHL's Rookie of the Year. He became the youngest player in league history to win these honors.

At the annual NHL awards luncheon in 1967, New York Ranger Harry Howell received the James Norris Trophy as the league's best defenseman. When he accepted the award, Howell said, "I'm glad I won this award now because I've got a feeling that from now on it's going to belong to Bobby Orr."

Despite Bobby's fine individual performance, Boston finished in last place. Bruin fans were not too disappointed. They knew better days were ahead.

An important trade during the off-season brought Phil Esposito, Ken Hodge and Fred Stanfield to Boston from the league-leading Chicago Black Hawks. Bobby and his new teammates were fired up. They wanted to win. The 1967-68 season ended with Boston in third place. For the first time in 9 years the Bruins had qualified for the Stanley Cup playoffs.

During the season Bobby had injured his left knee. He was operated on in February and later returned to the line-up for the playoffs. Unable to pivot properly, Bobby contributed little to the Bruin cause. The Montreal Canadiens manhandled the Boston team, winning all 4 play-off contests.

Although he had played in only 46 of Boston's 74 games, Bobby was named to the First All-Star team. As Harry Howell had predicted, the James Norris Trophy was awarded to Bobby. He was well on his way to becoming a superstar.

During his second season Bobby learned a great many things which helped him to mature both as a hockey player and as a man.

In a game against the Maple Leafs, Toronto's Brian

Conacher hit Bobby in the face with his stick. The blow broke Bobby's nose. Bobby was angry because he thought Conacher had hurt him on purpose.

Bobby knocked Conacher down and began pounding him viciously with his fists. When the fight was stopped, both men were covered with blood.

Bobby was sent to the penalty box. When Bobby returned to the ice, he found he couldn't grip his stick properly. He had sprained his thumb during the fight.

Boston sportswriters criticized Bobby for losing his temper. One newspaperman pointed out that a superstar is of no help to his team sitting in the penalty box or missing games due to injuries caused by fighting.

It was the first criticism Bobby had ever received from the Boston press. The criticism angered him. Bobby thought he had been justified in fighting back this time. He knew very well how rough the NHL is. "You've got to protect yourself," he said. "If they see you backing away, you're finished."

The criticism did serve one very good purpose. It proved to Boston sportswriters and fans and even to Bobby himself that he was human after all.

Then Bobby began to relax. The shy, self-conscious boy who had insisted upon calling his teammates "Sir" began to get to know his fellow Bruins better.

The naive kid who had always answered reporters' questions in a bland and overly humble way began to speak out thoughtfully and candidly.

The rookie who had wept when he played a bad game started to gain a more mature perspective. Bobby began to develop an engaging sense of humor.

Though he changed and began to assert his personality, Bobby remained an essentially polite and modest young man.

After the 1967-68 season a second operation was performed on Bobby's left knee. He spent the summer in Parry Sound recuperating.

When training camp opened for the 1968-69 season, Bobby's knee was not yet strong enough for him to practice with the team; but when the season began, he was skating as well as ever.

One of the greatest games in his career came on December 16, 1968, against the Chicago Black Hawks. On that historic night Bobby became the second defenseman in NHL history to score a 3-goal hat trick. Former Bruin, Eddie Shore, the greatest defenseman of all time until Bobby came along, had also performed the feat.

Late in the season the Bruins held first place in the

East Division. Then Bobby twisted his bad knee and had to miss 9 games. When he was able to play again, the Bruins had fallen to second place.

Bobby finished the season with 21 goals and 43 assists. Both were new league records for a defenseman. Once again Bobby was awarded the Norris Trophy. He repeated as a First Team All-Star.

In the Stanley Cup play-offs that year the Bruins

managed to reach the semifinals, only to be ousted again by the Canadiens.

In his first 3 years as a Bruin Bobby had done everything expected of him except spark his team to a Stanley Cup victory. However, Boston fans felt that victory wouldn't be long in coming.

When training camp opened for the 1969-70 season, the Bruins were confident that this would be their year to

go all the way. Then a tragic accident put everything in doubt.

During an exhibition game, team leader Ted Green was struck on the head by a puck flying at over 100 miles per hour. His skull was fractured, and for a time it looked as though he might not live. Green stubbornly clung to life and finally recovered. But he missed the entire season.

The injury to Green thrust 21-year-old Bobby into the unfamiliar role of team leader. He quickly showed that he had leadership ability.

Bobby went on to have perhaps the greatest season any NHL player has ever had. At the end of regular season play Bobby had recorded 33 goals, breaking his own record for defensemen. His 87 assists were the most ever made in a single NHL season by any player, regardless of position. Bobby's total of 120 points led the league—the first time a defensemen had ever taken the NHL scoring title.

Most important of all, the Bruins had won the Stanley Cup at last, defeating the St. Louis Blues in the finals. Bobby's overtime goal in the fourth game of the series clinched it for the Bruins. In 14 play-off games Bobby had 9 goals and 11 assists, an incredible performance.

Sipping champagne from the historic Stanley Cup was a great thrill for Bobby. He and the Bruins were on top of the hockey world.

Bobby received the Hart Trophy as the NHL's Most Valuable Player. He won his third straight Norris Trophy. He was named to the First All-Star team for the third consecutive year.

There were other honors as well. Bobby was awarded the Art Ross Trophy as the league's leading scorer. He was voted the Conn Smythe Trophy as the Most Valuable Player in the play-offs. *Sports Illustrated* magazine voted Bobby Sportsman of the Year for 1970.

At 22, an age when most players are just getting started, Bobby was already the best all-round player in the NHL. Hockey experts generally rated Bobby the greatest defenseman hockey has ever known.

There was no longer any question about Bobby's greatness. All that was left to be determined was whether or not he was the greatest player of all time.

Bobby Orr's style has revolutionized the game. Even great players like Gordie Howe have studied his technique.

Something special happens when Bobby is on the ice. He dominates the game in a way that no other player in history has done. New York Ranger Brad Park once said, "When Bobby's on the ice, you're playing against an extra man."

Bobby has established the standard by which defensive excellence is measured today. It is a perfect combination of offense and defense. Not only does Bobby lead the attack up the ice, he speeds back to defend the Bruin goal. He often blocks speeding shots with his body, deflecting the puck to the sideboards.

Bobby skates and stick-handles better than most forwards. He is equally effective playing right-handed or left-handed. His slapshot, one of the hardest and most accurate in hockey, travels at over 110 miles per hour.

Bobby has what the pros call "puck sense." He seems to know instinctively where the puck is and where it's going to be.

Bobby's moves and fakes are legend. When Bobby was a rookie, Ted Green said, "He's got moves that take the rest of us 5 years to pick up." Every season Bobby seems to come up with something more spectacular.

Bobby has instant acceleration as a skater. He's able to change speeds at will, shifting from high to low in mid-ice. His numerous lateral shifts and reverse spins make him extremely difficult to catch.

Defenseman Jim Neilson of the New York Rangers says, "You think you've got him lined up for a check, and . . . whoosh . . . he's gone again."

Though small by NHL standards—5-feet-11 and 185 pounds—Bobby is an exceedingly strong and effective checker. Bobby Hull, perhaps the greatest shooter in hockey history, once said, "Running into Orr is like getting hit by a pick-up truck."

Bobby spends more time on the ice than any other Bruin. He has great desire to be in the game, even when injured. One of Bobby's opponents, referring to Orr's injured knee, has said, "He's better on one leg than most players are on two."

Over the years Bobby has gained remarkable composure and maturity. He fights less than he used to. He spends fewer minutes in the penalty box than before. He's a smarter player now than he was when he first entered the NHL. "I have found out," Bobby says, "that you can save a lot of energy by being smart on the ice, by passing the puck more."

In his next 3 seasons, 1970-1973, Bobby continued to live up to his reputation. During the 1970-71 campaign he scored 139 points including 102 assists, a new NHL record. In 1971-72 he helped the Bruins recapture the coveted Stanley Cup. Though he was injured for part of the 1972-73 season, Bobby still finished with 101 points.

He was named to the First All-Star team and received the Norris Trophy all 3 of those years. Twice he won the Hart Trophy. In 1972 he won his second Conn Smythe award.

During those years Bobby continued to have trouble with his left knee. He often missed games or played injured. Bobby knows that another serious knee injury could end his career. He says, "Hockey is my life, and you can't survive for long with a bad knee."

Bobby got off to a flying start during the 1973-74 season. Then at mid-season he reinjured his knee. Bobby sat on the sidelines, his career very much in doubt; but he said he would be back before the season ended. Bruin fans were not inclined to doubt him.

JACK NICKLAUS
BILL RUSSELL
MARK SPITZ
VINCE LOMBARDI
BILLIE JEAN KING
ROBERTO CLEMENTE
JOE NAMATH
BOBBY HULL
HANK AARON
JERRY WEST
TOM SEAVER
JACKIE ROBINSON
MUHAMMAD ALI
O. J. SIMPSON
JOHNNY BENCH
WILT CHAMBERLAIN
ARNOLD PALMER
A. J. FOYT
JOHNNY UNITAS
GORDIE HOWE

superstars! superstars! superstars!

CREATIVE EDUCATION SPORTS SUPERSTARS

WALT FRAZIER
PHIL AND TONY ESPOSITO
BOB GRIESE
FRANK ROBINSON
PANCHO GONZALES
LEE TREVINO
KAREEM ABDUL JABBAR
JEAN CLAUDE KILLY
EVONNE GOOLAGONG
ARTHUR ASHE
SECRETARIAT
ROGER STAUBACH
FRAN TARKENTON
BOBBY ORR
LARRY CSONKA
BILL WALTON
ALAN PAGE
PEGGY FLEMING
OLGA KORBUT
DON SCHULA
MICKEY MANTLE